A GOLD ORCHID

1 (*Frontispiece*). "Bamboo in the Wind," by P'u Ming, 14th century. *Courtesy of the Cleveland Museum of Art, John L. Severance Fund.*

A GOLD ORCHID

The Love Poems of Tzu Yeh

translated from the Chinese by

Lenore Mayhew & William McNaughton

CHARLES E. TUTTLE COMPANY
Rutland, Vermont & Tokyo, Japan

Representatives

For Continental Europe:
BOXERBOOKS, INC., *Zurich*

For the British Isles:
PRENTICE-HALL INTERNATIONAL, INC., *London*

For Australasia:
PAUL FLESCH & CO. PTY., *Melbourne*

For Canada:
M. G. HURTIG, LTD., *Edmonton*

*Published by the Charles E. Tuttle Company, Inc.
of Rutland, Vermont and Tokyo, Japan
with editorial offices at
Suido 1-chome, 2-6, Bunkyo-ku, Tokyo*

*Copyright in Japan, 1972
by Charles E. Tuttle Co., Inc.*

*Library of Congress Catalog Card No. 72-79019
International Standard Book No. 0-8048 0211-4*

First printing, 1972

PRINTED IN JAPAN

TABLE OF CONTENTS

LIST OF ILLUSTRATIONS

ACKNOWLEDGMENTS

We would like to acknowledge the help of the following: the Trustees of Oberlin College, Oberlin, Ohio, who, with an H. H. Powers Travel Grant, made possible some of the basic research for the book; Mr. Keith Botsford, director, and the National Translation Center, who with a grant made possible residence abroad and consultation on linguistic and textual problems; the Chinese literature faculty of Kyoto University; the office of the president, Kyoto University, and the gardeners in the Taipei Botanical Gardens.

We would also like to thank the following publishers for their permission to use quotations from several poems: J. M. Dent & Sons Ltd., London; Harcourt, Brace & World, Inc., New York; MacGibbon & Kee Ltd., London; New Directions Publishing Corporation, New York; Oxford University Press, New York; and Arnoldo Mondadori Editore, Milan.

INTRODUCTION

The "Music Section" of the *T'ang History* says: "The 'Tzu Yeh Songs' are Chin dynasty [A.D. 265–420] songs. During the Chin, there was a woman called Tzu Yeh, who made these songs. They sing surpassingly of grievance and grief." The "Music Section" of the *Sung History* gives bibliographical information according to which we can date Tzu Yeh as "latter half of the fourth century [A.D.]."

The *Yueh-fu Shih-chi* [Anthology of Music Bureau Poems], Chapter 44, has 117 poems entitled "Tzu Yeh Poems," plus a miscellany of poems, attributed to other people, which are imitative of her work. Two of these 117 poems are assigned in *The Jade Terrace Anthology*, Chapter 10, to the Liang dynasty (A.D. 503–51) "Martial Emperor." That leaves 115 poems that have been, one way or another, attached to her name.

Why Translate Tzu Yeh?

It was fashionable a few years ago, before a computer was made available to the Columbia University Classics Department, to say that the Homeric poems were written by different people. So is it fashionable now to say that a lot of other people, not Tzu Yeh, wrote the Tzu Yeh poems. But whether or not there was "a real Tzu Yeh," the Tzu Yeh poems represent an entire period of Chinese poetry—between the Han and Sui dynasties [A.D. 221–589]—which has been neglected in the West. The Tzu Yeh poems are one of the period's most important coherent bodies of work. Chinese anthologies always give exceptional play to them. Major Chinese poets (among them the Liang "Martial Emperor," Wang Han, and Li Po) admired Tzu Yeh's poems sufficiently to imitate them.

Apart from the great beauty of these poems, and the astounding originality of some of them, they are especially important in the history of Chinese verse for the following two reasons: (1) they are written in the five-syllable line (*wu-yen shih*) at just about the time that that line asserted the dominance which it was to hold for a long time thereafter; (2) they are in the quatrain form and so stand as a major base for the T'ang dynasty's poetry (Lu K'an-ju says, "In the T'ang, they wrote mostly quatrains"). The Tzu Yeh poems also stand as important antecedents to one of the two most rigorous classical Chinese verse forms, the *chüeh-chü*.

What Do We Know About Tzu Yeh?

We know about Tzu Yeh, really, only what is translated above from the *T'ang History*—and what the poems tell us. We worked on her poems every day for almost two years, and we suppose she was a wineshop girl. If she was a wineshop girl, it would account for the subjects and scenes of which she writes, and would explain (which is less easy) her considerable poetic skill (see On Translating Tzu Yeh, p. 125). Wineshops were an important institution in the Orient; like any important institution, they loom large in the literature. They are still important in China and Thailand, and the wineshop girl today endures in Japan as the geisha or geiko, and the maiko.

What sort of institution is the wineshop, and how does it work? If a Chinese wants to entertain you at dinner, he probably will not invite you to his house. He instead will reserve a room in his favorite restaurant, and the entertainment will take place there, professionally prepared and served. Suppose he rather wants to give a party—the Oriental equivalent of the cocktail party, say. He can invite you and his friends to a wineshop, or "winehouse" as they really are called in Chinese. The winehouse will furnish your party with a room, wine, snacks, and professional entertaining girls. The girls will talk, pour your wine, play party games, dance, and maybe sing for you. A better winehouse has its own small combo (usually with Western instruments today), which will visit your party, if you like, and play awhile for you. Onto your host's bill will go food and wine consumed, service, the girls' time, and music if any. You are entitled to the girls' company and conversation, and that is all.

The entertaining-girls, or "wineshop girls," are no more, or no less, sexually "accessible" than other unattached professional women. Some of them are engaged, and a few marry very well—particularly in Japan, where the geisha and maiko receive a training that is long and difficult, and where they contribute a good deal more to national recreation than do café singers or movie stars. The wineshop girl of early centuries—particularly if she were beautiful and skillful enough to enjoy special status—had quite the same freedom of choice about her lovers, and even about her clients. The main difference in the institution, as it flourished in ages past and as it flourishes now, is that the girls lived in the winehouse in earlier ages, and received lovers there if they wished. They were also often in debt to the "mama-san" (as she is called now in both China and Japan) for their clothes and, more importantly, for their training. It is still quite an expensive proposition to train and to outfit a geisha, and that is probably the main reason why "wineshop entertainment" is on a higher level in Japan than in China: in Japan, they receive a real professional training. Alas, none of the girls seem to compose poetry impromptu (or promptu) anymore, although they did in the T'ang dynasty and probably did in Tzu Yeh's day. Literary skill—the ability to versify—was, in fact, one of the necessary talents, traditionally. The Sung-dynasty story, "The Oil-Peddler and the Queen of Flowers," says of its heroine, "By the time she was fourteen, Meiniang was a very beautiful girl. The rich and aristocratic young men of Linan sought her company. They came willing to pay well, some to enjoy her beauty, some to get examples of her accomplished verse or calligraphy."

The Tzu Yeh Poems

The Tzu Yeh poems give us a very clear idea of this life, of its sorrows and its compensations. They also give us what was assumed not to exist when missionaries were doing all the translating—Chinese erotic poetry. (It was considered nonexistent despite the fact that a Chinese emperor had even had an anthology of it collected for him, and called it *The Jade Terrace Anthology*.) But significant linguistic work has been done in recent years on the poetic vocabulary, and we now have the work of Clement Egerton, of Lau She, and of R. H. Van Gulik to build on, so that terms like "jade terrace," "jade stalk," "gold hibiscus," and so on need not mislead our judgment, or confuse our understanding.

How were the Tzu Yeh poems recorded and preserved? We have the poems because the Chinese, even millennia ago, collected and preserved the nation's poetry. They did not do it simply for the convenience of lovers of poetry, however, or out of responsibility to the life of the mind. The imperial government had to keep in touch with the people's temper and spirit, even to the remote provinces of the empire, so it collected folksongs and used them to read the people's feelings and moods. During the Han dynasty (206 B.C.–A.D. 221), the emperor established—some say "re-established"—a "Music Bureau" to collect, to edit, and to interpret these songs. We have Tzu Yeh's poems because the Music Bureau did this work, and because the best of what they collected was published and preserved.

In *The Music Bureau Anthology*, the Tzu Yeh poems are arranged in five sections: "Tzu Yeh Songs," and "Tzu Yeh Four-Season Songs" which are subdivided into Spring, Summer, Autumn, Winter. We have not followed this organization in our book. We have tried to arrange the poems, rather, so that they tell the lady's story or, if there was no lady or were many ladies, so that the poems present, in Browning's phrase, "incidents in the development of a soul." We have used our historical material, which is the poetic texts, to make a fictional, or if you like, poetical, history. The poems, in any case, present an image of some part of that age, and we hope that our arrangement of them accords with Ernst Robert Curtius's vision: "Our survey of the modern historical method has led us to the concept of poetry in the sense of a narrative produced by the imagination ('fiction') [*Unser Blick auf die Moderne Geschichtswissenschaft hat uns zum Begriff* *der Dichtung im Sinne einer von der Phantasie geschaffenen Erzählung* (fiction) *geführt*]."* It would seem to make better sense, or at least more interesting reading, than to put a nineteen-year-old girl's poem beside a forty-five-year-old woman's, simply because they both were written in winter.

The title *A Gold Orchid* comes from the second section of the book, which presents what seems to be the main drama of Tzu Yeh's (as of many a girl's) life: the search for "Mr. Right." A "gold orchid friend," in Chinese, is one's special soulmate, or "the other half of one's tally-stick," and Tzu Yeh tried very hard to find hers. For the rest of it, the section "Washing Stone" may be obscure, and we cannot say whether she really was married for a while, or whether—like the Captain's mistress—she merely wished for it, and fantasized about it.

*   *   *

The Tzu Yeh poems do not much lend themselves to annotation. They belong, as we have said, to "Music Bureau," or nonscholarly, verse. The notes below some of the poems are given as a record of problems we have met in making these translations. Some of the problems we solved by referring to dictionaries of one sort or another; others, by visiting

* Ernst Robert Curtius, *Europäische Literatur und lateinisches Mittelalter* (Bern and Munich, 1948), p. 18. Trans. Willard Trask. (Where no other translators are identified, all translations are by Lenore Mayhew and William McNaughton.)

art galleries in the United States, Japan, and Nationalist China; others, by walking through the Taipei Botanical Garden and pestering the gardeners with questions; and still others, by asking other scholars or specialists. We include in the notes some information which is already well known to sinologists, but which less advanced students—who, we hope, may find this book useful—may not know. We do not feel that the notes really "elucidate" the poems; a poem must generate its own light. But notes should make it easier for scholars to see where we have gone wrong, and to specify our errors.

THE TRANSLATORS

I

CINNAMON WINE

2. "Two Doves on a Flowering Branch," Anonymous, 12th–13th century. *Courtesy of the Smithsonian Institution, Freer Gallery of Art, Washington D.C.*

Cinnamon Wine

SHINING winds flow over
           an edge of moon,
Budding trees unroll
           bright brocade flowers.
Tender people play
           in spring's night,
Trailing slender hands
           from silk sleeves.

CALLING night-birds
       cry in the bamboo wood.
Falling plum flowers
       fill the moonlit paths.
A pleasing lady
       strolls in the spring night,
Gauze hem dragging
       in the scented grass.

SPRING flowers
       seductive thoughts
Spring birds
       sad thoughts
Spring winds
       (chaotic thoughts)
Blow open
       my silk net skirt.

Moon bright
in the high
star sky,

Spring night
and the cool
wind rises.

Orchid house,
and they quarrel
as they pretty and prepare—

Behind lace curtains
someone waiting
once again to be
                    love-stirred.

Orchid house: the women's quarters. In classical Chinese, there are
several substantives which often appear as adjectives with only a remote
reference to the original substance. They mean about the same thing as
"fair" or "sweet" in Elizabethan poetry. Among these substantives are
"orchid," "jade," "fragrance," and—sometimes—"gold." "Jade" is
probably the most common.

W̲ID̲E̲ scarlet halls
                    are open to the air
And circled
              by the moat-hibiscus.
There, a jade bed, carved
                    like delicate bamboo—
A likely spot
          for tangled kisses.

Moat-hibiscus: *fu-jung*. This refers either to the lotus *Nelumbo nucifera* or to the tree-hibiscus *Hibiscus mutabilis*. The *Nelumbo nucifera* grows in water, has large round leaves that rise above the water on long stems, and produces large pink or white flowers. The *Hibiscus mutabilis* grows about 10 feet high and the flowers are pink or white.

During summer 1967, the Old Palace Museum in Taipei had an exhibit of circular fan-paintings of the Sung dynasty, which included paintings both of the lotus and of the tree-hibiscus. In Feng Ta-yu's "Lotus in the Wind" painting the flowers were pink or white, and the plant had tall stems with leaves growing several inches above the water. The exhibit also included an anonymous fan painting of hibiscus in which the plant had a leaf like a geranium, and the flowers were white grading into pink, and pink grading into red. According to the gardeners in the Taipei Botanical Garden, this color gradation on the flowers is one reason why the hibiscus is so much prized. Perhaps because of its ambiguity, the term *fu-jung* has passed from current usage and has been replaced by "tree-hibiscus" for the *Hibiscus mutabilis* and by *ho* or *fu-ch'ü* for the *Nelumbo nucifera*. The hibiscus grows in marshy ground, and various types of it are called rose mallow, rose of Sharon, and marsh mallow in English. (The latter word, of course, has been spoiled for poetry by the confectioners.) Since the *Nelumbo nucifera* and the *Hibiscus mutabilis* grow in similar environments and resemble each other, it is not surprising that the terms should be confused. The

JADE tower's dark
in the new moon,

Gauze lace, lowered
in the fresh wind.

We savor spring, and never
finish singing,

Faces crimsoned
by the cinnamon wine.

translator's task is much complicated by such linguistic perversities,
or vitalities.

It is interesting to note that the mallow in European poetry, too, has
erotic or amatory significances. See Rocco Scotellaro, "È Caldo Così
La Malva": "There's left / in my / bed the / odor / of your / body. //
It's warm / like the / mallow / we store / to dry / against / winter's /
evils." (Trans. W.M. By permission of the publishers, Arnoldo
Mondadori Editore, Milan.)

Tower: lou. This is a very troublesome word to translate. The Chinese
idea of the architectural "fundamental division" is: (1) houses of one
storey; (2) storeyed houses; the lou is the storeyed house. The novel
Hung-lou Meng (mistranslated as Dream of the Red Chamber) has this word
lou in its title to signify wealth or wordly glory, since only the rich
lived in storeyed homes. The wineshops also had a second storey, where
the girls lived, slept, and perhaps received lovers. The Old Palace Mu-
seum in Taipei has a long scroll, "The River-festival," in which a
storeyed wineshop is depicted, and the girls can be seen upstairs
helping a drunken customer into bed.

THEY are soft and radiant
    and dance
        gracefully,

Turning now here,
    now there; and when
        they sing again,

Bright robes
    of blossoming flowers
        will fall

And thoughts of home
drop from men's minds.

RAISING wine,
        each waits and urges.
Wine repaid
        leaves empty cups.
Just before the click of crystal,
Like desires
        already touch.

ELEGANT, graceful,
she lifts her sleeves
to dance.

Slender and soft,
Her supple body
turns.

By the standing
candle, in the orchid
light,

Her face seduces
and the spring winds
rise.

Spring winds: this term refers both to spring wind and to sexual de-
sire, "the tempestuous wind that never rests," as Dante calls it
(*Inferno* 5, 31; trans. W.M.). Dante's creative act or insight in this pas-
sage sharpens and specializes an old image of wind, relating it specifi-
cally to sexual desire; this corresponds to a built-in metaphor of early
Chinese poetry.

He tries
to lift
the brocade hem

When once again
the crossed
sleeves part.

The lowered
belt
has come untied

And gauze
and net's
soon pulled aside.

COAL stove
drives off the late
night-chill

As, double-
robed, on folded
quilts,

We sit
facing, on the flowered
bed.

Strings sing,
and I touch the orchid
candle.

Touch: there may be a pun on the homonymous word for "bright"—
"Strings sing, and the orchid candle is bright." And in fact there is a
textual variant which gives the word "bright" here. In that version,
the "direction" of the pun would be reversed.

Ｎ E W grass
edges
the long road.

Red pepper
weights
the jade stalk.

Winds flow
over
the wide fields,

Each breeze
delighting
in the flower-play.

COOL autumn
   and the windows opened wide
Low moon
   and the slanted lights inside.

Midnight
  nothing heard,
    nothing seen
A double laugh
   behind the screen.

AUTUMN moon's
   at the open shutter.
The light's put out,
   sheer robe's gone wide.
Within silk curtains
   someone smiles;
The lifted orchid's come untied.

HIGH-FLYING clouds
   are packed with ice,
And snow piles
   on the stiffening stream
Where touching hillsides
   tie the crystal peak
And jasper branches shake
   in the raked courtyard.

THE mist-puffs rise
beneath the moon,

Beside the lake,
night-crickets whirr.

The nenuphar
adds folded leaves

And stretches out
before it flowers.

Nenuphar: i.e., *fu-jung*. (See fn., p. 28.) We have used an image to
dodge Tzu Yeh's pun. Puns do not translate anyway: see Frost, and see
Pound on logopoeia (discussed on p. 126, below). The last distich in
the Chinese runs "*Fu-jung* begins to tie on leaves. / The flower's splen-
dor has not yet formed lotus fruit." The Chinese poem is carried by
the word "lotus fruit" (*lien*), which is homonymous to the word
meaning "be moved/love/lover" (*lien*). This lotus fruit/lover pun is a
favorite one of this period, and Tzu Yeh uses it more than once. She
also puns *lien* ("lover") with other words. See fns., pp. 59 and 64.

B ACK and forth he goes
                    on bamboo flowers,
As yet unable to unlatch
                    the outside screens—
A bold lord,
                    caught inside this place
Until I've put on clothes
                    and fixed my face.

Bamboo flowers: students have asked, "What are the bamboo flowers and what is their significance?" They are the same as the flowers in William Carlos Williams's poem "The Nightingales," and their significance is the same: "My shoes as I lean / unlacing them / stand out upon / flat worsted flowers. // Nimbly the shadows / of my fingers play / unlacing / over shoes and flowers." (*Collected Earlier Poems,* p. 130. Copyright 1938 by William Carlos Williams; reprinted by permission of New Directions Publishing Corp., New York, and MacGibbon & Kee Ltd., London.)

   A young poet, a student of Theodore Roethke's from the Pacific Northwest, once asked Pound "what the cat was a symbol of," in "Desolate is the roof where the cat sat. / . . . / And the cornerpost / whence he greeted the sunrise,"* and Pound said, "Sometimes KATZ is KATZ, and FRAWGS is FRAWGS." Anyone who has visited Venice knows what a feature of the city cats are. (*The Cantos of Ezra Pound,* "Eleven New Cantos," p. 43. Copyright 1934 by Ezra Pound, reprinted by permission of New Directions Publishing Corp., New York.)

FOLDING up the fan,
           she puts it on her bed
Attentive to the stir of distant winds.
Light sleeves wide
           against her gay gauze dress,
With graceful steps,
           she climbs the highest stairs.

SPRING'S wind makes a spring heart.
Idle eyes linger on the hills and trees.
Hills and trees bedazzle with their brilliancies
And mating birds erupt in raucous song.

3. "Bamboo in the Moonlight," by Su Shih, 1037–1101.
*Reprinted, by permission, from "T'ang, Sung, and Yüan Paintings
Belonging to Various Chinese Collectors," by Berthold Laufer
(Paris and Brussels: G. Van Oest and Co., 1924).*

Washing Stone

RED lights glow in the green-black garden—
Scarlet flowers under a net of stars.
Strange if someone sits inside and sews,
Alone insensitive
                    to spring's desires.

MULBERRY leaves
are gone by spring.

When summer begins,
the silk is spun.

Day and night,
she ties the loom

And hopes the matching's
quickly done.

It's feed, feed
the silkworms,
and after—

Although nerves
ache, this
gentle wife

Who knows
that travelers
need clothes

Weaves, weaves
on just
the hottest days.

Gentle wife: literally, "thoughtful wife," or "wife thinking of her man, missing him." The word for "thoughtful/thought" is homonymous to that for "silk." The pun "silk/thoughts (of you)" became popular in Chinese poetry, and much was made of the implication, "our thoughts bind us together, like threads of silk." Tzu Yeh no doubt intended the pun here.

A CLEAR wind comes
to cool the air.

A bright moon hangs
in the high sky.

A beautiful girl
prepares the winter clothes,

Working, club against stone,
stitch by stitch.

W HEN sunlight's gone
        the white dew gathers,
Night-freezing in September's wind.
Remember him who waits for winter clothes
And in the moonlight
        beat the raw silk.

W INTER'S wild geese
        find the South.
Flying swallows
        seek the North.
Would God I knew
        where my warrior walks—
"Follow the autumn wind
        and come home."

The second line of this poem has only four characters. The line begins
with a textual note: "There's a character missing here."

WINTER'S here—
October,
November.

By myself
I bind the
unreeled silk.

Winter's clothes
are not yet
stitched and hemmed.

Tall men call
me "love," and
I work on.

BRIGHT moon
lights up the cinnamon
woods

And colors opening flowers
in shades of amber
like a gold brocade.

I think of
you—how
should I not?

—As, lonely
on my loom,
I weave.

THIS wide-cheeked face
          has strange appeal,
Much more so
          as her blush moves higher.
Now warm winds stir the southern screens,
This weaving wife
          feels spring's desire.

4. "Pink Hibiscus," by Li Ti, active 12th century. *The Tokyo National Museum.*

Rose Hibiscus

THE sun goes down. I reach my gate.
You pass. I stand and stupid stare—
Those thick side-curls, that melting face,
That penetrating perfume, filling up the air!

P ERFUME
is just
an aggregate

Of smells,
and such a face
avoids

Commitments.
Those gods
dislike

A settled
vow,
who send you now.

AT the open
window, I
stand and scowl

With belt
untied, and dragging
sleeves.

Since net
moves easily
in wind,

If my dress
parts, blame
spring's breeze.

The last line puns on the secondary meaning of "spring's breeze"
("desire": see fn., p. 31). This pun on a phrase is an interesting
illustration of Valéry's statement, "*les phrases deviennent à chaque in-
stant des mots* [phrases are always turning into words]."

NEW clouds roll
            in a high-colored spring.
Scented wind
            scatters the clustered flowers.
Now, in the garden,
            the beauty walks.
To her silk-worked sash,
                  petal-crowns cling.

IN thin silk dress
            red sleeves a-flutter
In crescent earrings
                  hairpin of jade
In restless melting mood
In steps across the dews of spring,
I stroll

A sensuous search
            for a bold someone
With a heart like mine.

I'M standing there
half-eaten peach
in hand

And handsome wants
to match his fan
to mine.

Match fans—
I think I
understand

And so I mention
"orchid rooms"
and "nine."

SUMMER earth
is windless. Heat
still presses.

Sparse clouds
cluster where night
skies come.

Thick leaves are
hiding two
joined hands

And the gaudy
gourd covers
the plum.

I'LL dig a pond
nine counties long

Around it build
the house I need,

Plant rose hibiscus
flower to flower

And easily seize
the mallow seed.

Rose hibiscus: i.e., *fu-jung*. See fn., p. 28.
Mallow seed: Tzu Yeh is again punning on *lien*. See fn., p. 37.

THINKING of
a chance to play
at moon and flowers,

I assume
a smile, and find
a public road.

Here comes one
I know'd undress me
if he could. . . .

What a pity—
he doesn't
think he should.

W HIRL, whirl
in autumn's evening

Fire-dazzled
by September's moon.

Catch his wrist
in teasing play

And flatter up
this faint-heart, till he stay.

September: there is some chance of error in transposing times from the Chinese calendar to specific units in the Western calendar (the Chinese here actually says "early autumn"). We do it occasionally in the belief that, in poetry translations, the word most homely, germane, or familiar to the reader is likely to be the best.

SYMPATHY, desire
and love—
these feelings I'll embrace.

I'm going to move
my house
to a country place.

All along my fence
the saplings
will spring up,

And just before
my gate,
the striplings strut.

To feel desire
as summer's heat

Three summers' heat,
and be alone as now;

And then to brush the jade mat
with a scented cloth

And take the fellow up
into the tower.

Three summers: this expression in Chinese is actually an ellipsis for
"the three months of summer," but we liked the hyperbole of the
literal translation, so we let it stand.

GREEN lotus

     on the clear blue waves—
The blossom-crowns

     are red and new.
This guy is out

     to gather buds. . . .
"I'll give my

     passion flower

          to you."

Green lotus: Tzu Yeh calls the plant *ho* in line 1, *fu-jung* in line 2, and *lien* in line 4. (See fns., pp. 28 and 37.) The pun *lien*/lotus—*lien*/lover is there again. We have used a different tactic to try to get it this time. *Lien* is given in the earliest Chinese dictionary (*Erh-ya*) as "lotus fruit." The modern dictionaries note that *lien* has come simply to mean "lotus." The semantic shift already was taking place in Tzu Yeh's time. It could have taken place, in poetry or in lively language, anytime—by synecdoche. As translators, we have tried to let the total, particular poem guide us.

W HERE shall we tie together
        our two like desires?"

"On the western hillside,
        below the cypress trees,
Where razzle-dazzle sunrays
        will wall us all around."

"And harsh cold kill me
        on that frozen ground."

IT'S midsummer
and too hot to walk.

My thoughts
are tight as tangled silk.

I take a boat
and drift among the lilies

And scatter them
in Rose Hibiscus Lake.

Lilies: i.e., *lien*. The usual pun.
Rose Hibiscus: i.e., *fu-jung*. Tzu Yeh's line 3 ("and scatter them
in Rose Hibiscus Lake,") is our line 4, and vice versa.

THE harvest moon's extravagantly red.
The lady never leaves her fan.
This willowy jade-terrace girl
Walks willingly to play
          in the cold halls.

ANXIOUS and fretful,
       with longing for each other,
They begin to catch
       the wind from clouds.
The jeweled forest calls the high stone tower,
Two spirits
      paired by bitter thoughts.

T HEY see the girl and love
                    the face, the brow.
They'd like to spin
                "Gold Orchid" flower designs.
Lacking warp and woof
                we would weave in vain,
And it's hard to find
                a pattern matching mine.

Gold Orchid: see Introduction, p. 19.

Call (see last line on facing page): it would be in keeping with the style and practice of the period's poetry to assume that Tzu Yeh is punning on *huan* ("call") and *huan* ("joy, delight").

LET others
find themselves
alike,

My will
is obstinately
"I."

My winter
blinds are wide
to winds,

And long,
in cold, my curtains
fly.

PLUM flowers
                    are already lost.
Now willow flowers
                    follow the wind.
In such midmoments of the spring,
                    I sigh,
For whom do I desire, to call
                    "beloved"?

MY mind's a web of bitter thoughts.
I sigh, I grieve,
            tears stain my dress.
Why do I savor
            this disease,
Since no man
            knows enough to please?

JUST now the sea-green banners fly,
Late spring's already spilled away.
Forest magpies change to summer's tropes,
And from the wood, the loud cicadas cry

Sea-green banners: Dorothy McNaughton (aged 10) suggested that
the sea-green banners "must be the willow trees," and we were
satisfied with that explanation.

II

GOLD ORCHID

5. "Birds and Pine Tree," by Emperor Hui-tsung, 1082–
1135. *Reprinted, by permission, from "Chinese Painting," by
William Cohn (London: Phaidon Press, 1948).*

DOUBLE geese
In autumn's sky
make my

Delight,
spring's coupling
martins, joy.

But what new matches
can we see,
if eagles, seize

The prairie chick,
or the ringed-throat pheasant
die?

THE hours of the night are gone.
What time will find us here again?
The empty chessboard in the candle flame
Still waits,

for the chess game.

WILD winds whirl the young branches.
White sun draws the fine mists.
He wants to find a darkened room,
And I would lean

and bloom.

Wild winds: "the tempestuous wind." See fn., p. 31.

CLEAR dew becomes
a crystal frost.
At midnight
cool winds rise.
As yet, the one I like's
not come to sleep
And weak with love,
I walk with the bright moon.

ROADS are rough
and no
one travels,

But looking
for you
in the winter's cold

I go. You
don't
believe it?

Look:
footprints
in the snow.

In empty air

        the bright moon hangs.

Tonight, my lord and I will play:

His song

        with subtle thoughts

           wound round,

My singing

        with a woman's sound.

A woman's sound: the epithet in the last line is actually "fragrant" (*fang*), a wide word in classical Chinese. Depending upon the noun, it can mean "young, springtime, virtuous, amorous," and so on. In many expressions it refers or alludes to women.

Midnight—
in false frost
you come

And seeing you
I swiftly sing
complaints.

You lean to
kiss me in
the cold and dark

And autumn's
brilliance shines
through winter's ice.

Low skies
        are cold, as winter closes
With bitter winds' back-flying sleet.
Lovemaking under double quilts,
We know
        three summers' heat.

SHE has not
combed her hair
in days.

It falls
across her shoulders
and is caught

Around
the fellow's knee.
What place?

What place
does not require
our pity?

This poem, perhaps even better than the poems which depend on puns, shows what Pound means about logopoeia (see discussion on p. 126, below). The "kick" in this poem comes because Tzu Yeh really reverses her direction after the first line. "She has not combed her hair in days" sounds exactly like a poem about a lady separated from, or neglected by, her lover. There are dozens of such poems, so beginning. She's falling apart from too little loving. But the rest of the poem reverses the expectation.

SLEEPING, eating,
we always stay together.

Sitting, if one
rise, the other rises.

The lotus' jade
stalk, and the gold hibiscus—

Can they outlast
our ever-present love?

THIS hill-built hall
    has no
        high walls
And catches
    all four faces
        of the wind.
And when it
    blows your
        net robes wide,
I try to
    hide my
        sudden smile.

WHEN you must weep,
    then I am sad,
But if you laugh
    then I laugh, too,
Just like the pattern-following tree,
For like the root
    the branch will be.

Would you tie
fast this
special love?

Then look
in the
withered wood:

Pine and
fir are
seized by frost

Yet autumns, winters
come and go
with never a needle lost.

Pine and fir: the pine and fir ever have suggested to the Chinese true friendship, for they do not fall away during rough weather. Confucius's classic remark on friendship is, "When the year goes a-cold, we know pine and fir" (*Analects*, 9, 27).

Since my beloved went away
Dressing jars are tightly shut.
Disheveled hair
           stays disarrayed
And pretty powders
           in a row
                grow coats of yellow.

I remember
           desire like white light
And that you left
           as though you longed to stay.
Now, wispy mists
           half-hide the lotus flowers.
I see the blossoms
           but the color blurs.

Lotus: i.e., *fu-jung*. See fns., pp. 28 and 37.
Blossoms: *lien*. She's punning again. See fns., pp. 37 and 64.

AT dawn, I seek
the high, cool terraces.

At dark, I stay
among the orchid pools

To ride the wind
and pluck the wild hibiscus

And night by night
the thought of him, from dreams.

Wild hibiscus; i.e., *fu-jung*. See fns., pp. 28 and 37.
The last line has *lien* again: another pun.

YOU left
at spring's beginning.

Will you come
by autumn's end?

I hate these waters
flowing east

That never
westward bend.

SPRING's parting was
the end of spring.

Love's feelings last
like summer's heat.

For whom shall I lift skirts
behind the lace?

When shall we share again
paired pillows?

YOU left after
        the spring winds started.
You're back, with summer skies
                high and blue.
The long road's under
                a fast-going sun
But you'll delay
        anyway,
                isn't it true?

Light clothes! Few clothes!
No brocade for me!
These are hot and howling winds.
If these devil days of summer ever pass,
You've my promise—
I will powder

rouge

—and dress.

How often I'm afraid
        you have some double dream
When you've been long away
        from the clear stream.
How can our desires
        still be alike
If you follow muddy ditches
        like a withered pike?

So she grabbed you in the street
                and what could you do?
If you turn your back on me,
                it won't be something new.
Hinges soon sag on a wide-open door
And it won't fit tight
                as it did before.

I'm too young
to play these games—

False starts,
subterfuge, lies.

But you are like
unanchored duckweed

Changing every
shift of spring's wind.

I am
the North
Pole Star

That never, in a thousand
years,
will change or shift,

But you, beloved, have a heart
as movable
as the white sun's

That daily, east
to west
must drift.

Autumn winds
enter my window.

The lifted curtain
puffs and sways.

Raising my head,
I see the moon

And send affection
on its reaching rays.

Stripped branches
          wind-bend to the light.
White covering dew
          makes crystal frost.
The wish-weary traveler
          climbs to see
High-flying geese
          that cut the heart.

SLEEPLESS
in the long
night,

I toss
as drums beat out
the hour.

Since we
have no chance
to meet

My stomach's
sick
and sour.

SINCE he
left, that
eager guy,

Each day
how many
sighs I've sighed.

Bitter
phellodendron
makes this forest

And matches
by how much
my shaken heart.

Phellodendron: the *Phellodendron amurense*. The common name for the phellodendron is cork tree. It is a member of the rue family and is native to eastern Asia. The phellodendra are ornamental trees with "particularly attractive" aromatic foliage. They generally grow on hilly ground, reach a 30- or 40-foot height, and have an ash-white outer bark. In summer months, the phellodendra produce small yellow flowers. The flower, in autumn, ties on a round fruit "like a yellow bean," which, ripening, turns black. These abundant black fruits remain for a long time after the leaves have fallen.

Y OU'VE not come
and so I send this note.

Since you left,
I've not been out again.

Make a rose hibiscus,
brass or gold

And who could prize
the precious mallow-seed?

Rose hibiscus: i.e., *fu-jung*. See fns., pp. 28 and 37.
Mallow: *lien* (with the usual pun). See fns., pp. 37 and 64.

SORROW came
the hour that my
love left.

Never, I think,
will these re-echoing
sighs be done.

Yet even as a
yellow stump must
bloom in spring,

A bitter heart
still beats to each
day's sun.

YOU left as wild
geese
gathered on the bank.

You're back as swallows
build
along the bridge.

It's true, that harvest
moons
grow old

Only to bring
spring's
sudden sun.

Sun: the word used here is *yang*—the *yang* in "Yin-Yang theory." It
connotes the qualities male, light, hard, dry, warm, and assertive.
The image of "sun," obviously, suggests many of these qualities, but
the cultural connotations of translated words can never be exactly
parallel. Cf. fn., p. 106.

U P-TIEING tight this old love
　　　　　wishing and binding

Last year's threadlets strain and break
　　　　　rewinding the wish.

Shifting coming moods of spring,
　　　　　what new wishing will you bring,
Spring's spinning silkworms spin again
　　　　　what new thing?

Silk is silk
A wish—
　　　　　a wish once more.
Will this new thread
　　　　　wind and bind
Just as the old before?

UNABLE to swallow
she drops the chopsticks,
stumbling goes

To the inner room,
finds jasper pieces
and one by one

Dusts them up
and sets them by;
then arranges the board,

Wears out the time,
waits as she's waited
the chess-playing guy.

GRAB the pillow,
wait at our window.
Sleep, maybe.

When and if
this guy comes,
we really live.

Few pleasures
fewer excuses
God!

How many
times
can I forgive?

BIRDS coldly hang in the high tree,
Bitter winds scream in the withered wood.
Beloved, this total haggard melancholy's
Bound to do my looks great good.

IN deep water
            winter's ice
                    is three feet thick,
Crisp snow
            covers a thousand *li*.
My heart is like the cedar's changeless green,
But you, beloved,
            how do you
                    love me?

I wonder
where he's been—
this friend.

I much
dislike
a guarded face.

Three times
I speak—
no word from him.

And he calls
this "like
fir and pine"!

Friend; speak: the Chinese equivalents of these words are near-homo-
nyms, and the poet has punned on them. The third sentence, then,
has a secondary meaning: "If there are three 'beloveds,' then there is
no true response (no true match)." The "three," of course, is a
synecdoche for "several."

ONCE, we
shared our world
with ease.

But now,
how do
we live?

You turn
away, dislike
my hair—

Slow to desire,
is indifferent
to please.

SINCE first
my joy was all
your care

I cannot
say "Love goes" without
distress.

To overlay
the tortoise shell
with gold

Makes outer
beauty for an inner
worthlessness.

IN the early days of our affair,
Our two desires had one design.
But, patterned thread in a broken loom?
Imperfect silk is all you'll get.

On this high hill
plant mallow
flowers

Crisscross
the phellodendron
bank,

That we might have
an interlacing sweetness

To dissipate
what's sorrowful
and sour.

On this high hill . . . mallow: i.e., *fu-jung*. See fns., pp. 28, 37, and 94. Although the hibiscus, or mallow, is supposed to grow "in marshy ground," we also have seen them growing on high hills in Taiwan— e.g., Yüan Shan ("Round Mountain"), north of Taipei.
Phellodendron: see fn., p. 93.

No sleep
in the long night

Of white light
from the moon.

She thinks she hears
his voice, who's gone

And answers
to an empty room.

Hears his voice: the word *huan* ("call") occurs in this line. See fn.,
p. 68.

D A W N
leaving and thinking
        I pass through the front gate.

Evening
returning and thinking
        I ascend the rear slope.

Sighing, I ask
        to whom shall I speak?

In my woman's heart
        dark image of you.

The last line runs, "Within heart, darkly remember you." But the word for "darkly" is *yin*, the word for one of the two basic concepts in "Yin-Yang theory." *Yin* refers to the "feminine principle" in the universe, and all things dark, soft, damp, cool, yielding, "negative." Such "wide words" simply do not translate, and we have here split *yin* into "woman's" and "dark." We hope that is more effectively connotative.

I remember
a loving wild, wild
That pitied
neither
heels nor heads—
So rash, I
pulled the
double blinds.
Who knows what
goes, in
shuttered beds?

Heels nor heads: the dictionaries define *ch'ing-tao* as "to fall flat." It really means something like "to head-heel," or "to go head over heels." Note that, as Vladimir Mayakovsky told Roman Jacobson, in poetry the internal form of phrases, that is, the semantic load of their constituents, regains its pertinence—"even 'great' in *Great Bear*, or 'big' and 'little' in such names of Moscow streets as *Bolshaja Presnaja* and *Malaja Presnaja*." (See Jacobson's "Linguistics and Poetics," in *Style in Language*, ed. Thomas A. Sebeok [Cambridge, Mass., 1960] pp. 366–67.) It is more likely that Tzu Yeh is playing on the "head to heels" suggestion of it, than that she is using it only to mean "totally," or "flat without pity" (as in "I flat forgot it").
Double blinds: the word for blind, or curtain, is *lien*—homonymous to "lover, lovers"—and gives the poet another chance to pun. So that you get something like "Double lovers hold and cover each other." A Japanese scholar has suggested to us that in the last line, which runs "who knows allow thick thin," the poet may be still playing with the "curtain" idea. It is these layers on layers of meaning that make translation an interesting and even fascinating task.

NEWBORN swallows
  sing their practice tunes
As quarreling cuckoos
  call the coming day.
Shaping eyebrows,
  she forgets to paint her mouth
And garden-strolling
  walks desire away.

FROM the moment
  my love left,
What day's moment
  thought I not of love?
I fear the showering petals of spring
That never gain again the branch above.

Y OUR leaving
      makes these steady tears.
Your image
      brings this extreme grief.
How memory weakens knees,
        and bit by bit
Constant caring
      cuts away the heart.

I raise my head
      to look at *t'ung* trees.
Those flowers
      I love the most of all.
I wish that we had neither frost nor snow
And *t'ung* trees
      had a thousand years to grow.

T'ung trees: i.e., the *wu-t'ung* or *Firmiana plantanifolia*. The *wu-t'ung* is considered the national tree of China. In summer it puts on flowers that are yellow on white. The seed is edible, and the bark can be used to make cord.

BY spring's beginning
　　　　　joy was gone.
Cold misery's more
　　　　　by autumn's end.
In summer months
　　　　we "played with fire,"
And still I feel
　　　　that shared desire.

NORTH wind scatters
　　　　　snow and sleet,
Waters freeze
　　　　where green moats meet.
Seizing slender wrists, I go
To play the games
　　　　　of first-day snow.

W HEN roads are near, who counts the miles?
But now, you've reached a winter's distance,
And when will eastward moving water
Ever wind back west again?

Y OU left, with
spring grass
turning green.

You're back, the
porch is
piled with snow.

Who'd guess, you—
thinking'd
age me so—

White comes where
black hair
used to grow.

SNOW still stays
                on the dark ridge.
Redbud shines
                in the sunny wood.
Who need sound
                guitar or flute
When hills themselves
                are reed and lute?

III

TUNED LUTES

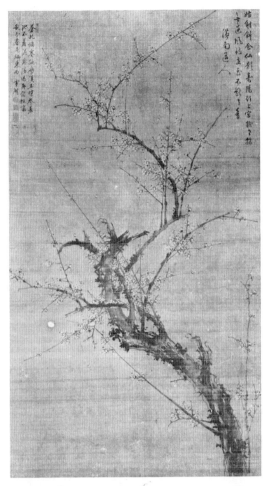

6. "An Old Plum Tree in Blossom," by Liu Shih-ju, active first half of the 16th century. *Courtesy of the Fogg Art Museum, Harvard University, Cambridge, Mass. Gift of Galen L. Stone.*

THIS spreading
splendor's
transient to trees,

Bare knots
and gnarls will hold
the autumn's frost.

Just now
we see these sudden
greening leaves,

Yet soon
spring's ninety days
are lost.

JUST now
        the early peach is red.
Will beauty mean
            that mine won't please—
But go unlooked for
And ungathered

As dropped flowers
        from midsummer trees?

MISTRUSTFUL and fretful,
I quarrel with time,

Moment by
moment, looking back.

In blossoming woodlands,
spring winds blow.

Always, I
fear scattering flowers.

IF forest flowers, all faded, fall
Another spring will make them bright,
Unless pulse scatter
        to perpetual shade
And leaning hearts be lost to light.

COMPASSION
for what's
bitter's

Denied
to innocents
of grief."

"And yet
one touch
of ice

Holds
all the winter's
cold."

Since years are few,
        let's seize the season.
Age comes
        when slipped days pass.
You must believe me
        now you see
Below the frost
        the once-green grass.

Bleak frosts gray the grass and trees.
Winter winds rise day and night.
That season comes when smiling ends in sighs.
Who dares to look—
        at hair gone white?

W E suddenly see
a heat-bright sun;
Cicadas sing
in winter air.
It's the season of sighing smiles
When black curls shine
in once-white hair.

W ALK, rewalk wild forest paths—
Their desolation silences the soul.
Yet spring's power makes winter pass:
Here's crocus, held in withered grass.

Yet spring's power makes winter pass: a literal translation of this line
would go: "Suddenly sing: greatly begins joy," and the flowers in the
last line line explain the joy and song. Cf. the troubadour Arnaut
Daniel's " . . . among first leaves / Bough and branch are new with
flowers. / . . . From my joy in them / I sing" (trans. W.M.).

Happy,
who does not
sing?

Hungry,
who does not
eat?

Dusk
comes, I lean against
the door:

Bitter,
who does not
remember?

NEWLY yellow
        grow the garden flowers.
Southern pools
        are just now turning green.
Someone begins
        to fill the cups with wine
And tuned lutes
        start the last twist.

SUDDENLY
it's
near-winter

And I
remember
April

Love,
the pleasure–chasing

And years,
passing
unnoticed.

ON TRANSLATING TZU YEH

As we translated Tzu Yeh, we tried to follow three modest general principles:

(1) to translate so that the reader, given differences between the geniuses of Chinese and English, still can get some idea of the original style and form;

(2) to translate so that the new version, in and of itself, can appeal to a reader's literary interest;

(3) to translate what the poet said, and not what we think she meant to say or what we would have said if we had written the poem instead—that is, to keep explanation and comment in the Introduction and footnotes.

In trying to find out exactly what the poet said, we have been helped enormously by recent linguistic and poetic research in Chinese, English, and Russian. We feel luckier than early translators in that we have had this work available to us. A list of helpful books appears in our bibliography, but two books should be singled out as especially important: Chou Fa-kao's work on grammar, and R. H. Van Gulik's work on lexicon.

In the following discussion of our method, we have found it helpful to use Ezra Pound's terms, *melopoeia*, *phanopoeia*, and *logopoeia*. As these terms are still not in general usage, a simple definition of each of them, as they are employed in Pound's *ABC of Reading*,* may be needed here. After describing literature as "language charged with meaning," Pound uses the terms to signify the "three possible ways" in which a poet can charge language with meaning: by the sound of words (melopoeia); by using words to project "a visual image on to the reader's imagination" (phanopoeia); and by using words "in some special relation" to their accustomed contexts (logopoeia). Pound's use of this last term implies an evocation by the poet of the associations and potential allusions of words, especially as they have been used by other poets.

Melopoeia

In trying to follow our first "general principle"—that is, that the translations should give some idea of the original style and form—we have been guided by the following specific principles:

(1) In working with the traditional ornaments *tieh-tzu* (iterated syllable), *tieh-yun* (rhyming compound), and *shuang-sheng* (alliterative compound), we have tried

* Norfolk, Conn.: New Directions, n.d., pp. 28, 36–38.

(a) where possible, to reproduce the same effect;

(b) where (a) is not possible, to convert the effect into one of the other two effects, e.g., an English alliterative compound (*shuang-sheng*) for a Chinese rhyming compound (*tieh-yun*);

(c) where necessary or advisable, to redefine the rhyming compound as a *compound accordé* and to use the Romains-Chennevière concept of *accord* instead of the conventional idea of rhyme; and

(d) if the Chinese ornament cannot be reproduced or imitated, to transpose the ornament to a contiguous or responsive demistich or metrum and so preserve at least the poem's "texture."* We have also tried

(2) to use rhyme

(a) wherever Tzu Yeh used it (a b c b) if we can, but

(b) to use it only so that it makes a better English poem; and

(3) to preserve the basic metrical pattern of 2 (pause) 3, but

(a) to substitute "beats" for syllables;

(b) to vary the basic pattern, according to the musical ideas of cola and of colotomic indication: three beats (pause) two beats; and also

(c) to vary the basic pattern, for special rhetorical or melopoetic effect, in one of two ways: using

(i) two beats (double pause) two beats (i.e., the musical rest); or

(ii) three beats (pause) three beats (i.e., musical "triplets").

---

* Cf. William McNaughton, "Pound's Translations and Chinese Melopoeia," *Texas Quarterly* 10, no. 4 (Winter 1967), pp. 52–56.

With regard to the melopoeia of Chinese verse, the traditional critics recognize as the three most important ornaments *tieh-tzu*, *tieh-yun*, and *shuang-sheng*. These are described below.

TIEH-TZU, OR ITERATED SYLLABLE

The iterated syllable occurs in most—maybe all—poetic language. Sister Miriam Joseph recognizes it as a feature of Shakespeare's poetic style:

> Out, out, brief candle!

And we can often find it in Dylan Thomas's work:

> Rage, rage against the dying of the light.*

Tzu Yeh uses this figure, for example, in the line, "*Heh heh sheng yang yueh*" (lit., "Red red is the full harvest moon").

TIEH-YUN, OR RHYMING COMPOUND

You find rhyming compounds much less often in English verse than in Chinese, and, so far as we know, the ornament is used more regularly, more consciously, in Chinese verse than in any other. (Quintilian, Demetrius, pseudo-Longinus, and pseudo-Cicero all fail to mention such an ornament.) A good example of the ornament and of its effect occurs in "The Windhover," by Gerard Manley Hopkins:

---

* "Do not go gentle into that good night," from *Collected Poems*, p. 123. Copyright 1952 by Dylan Thomas: reprinted by permission of New Directions Publishing Corp., New York; J.M. Dent & Sons Ltd., London; and the trustees for the copyrights of the late Dylan Thomas.

Fall, gall themselves, and gash gold-vermilion.*

Tzu Yeh has this ornament, for example, in the line, "*Yao t'iao yao t'ai nü*" (lit., "Fair, rare is the jeweled-terrace girl").

SHUANG-SHENG, OR ALLITERATIVE COMPOUND

The alliterative compound is different from simple alliteration. In the alliterative compound, two words already closely related by meaning or function are bound together even more closely by the alliteration. E. E. Cummings makes much use of this ornament in "All in Green Went My Love Riding":

> Softer be they than slippered sleep
> the lean lithe deer
> the fleet flown deer.†

Here is an example of the same ornament in Tzu Yeh:"*ch'ou ch'ang k'o hsin shang*" (lit., "Wish-weary, the traveler's heart is cut"). Tzu Yeh uses all three of these ornaments, not just in isolated instances, but as most Chinese poets do —as part of her style, regularly recurring.

Phanopoeia

Tzu Yeh often uses fairly obvious images that are, or were to become, the conventional images of Chinese poetry:

* *Collected Poems*, p. 12. Reprinted by permission of Oxford University Press, New York.
† *Poems 1923–54*, p. 124. Reprinted by permission of Harcourt, Brace & World, Inc., New York.

I fear the showering petals of spring
That never gain again the branch above.

[p. 108, above]

And the geese that occur in the poem below have become
routine in Chinese poetry; the Chinese poet, away from his
home, always sees geese going over and is saddened as he
watches them:

Stripped branches
                    wind-bend to the light.
White covering dew
                    makes crystal frost.
The wish-weary traveler
                    climbs to see
High-flying geese
                    that cut the heart.

[p. 91, above]

Tzu Yeh, on the other hand, can startle her reader with an
apt and far-fetched image or simile—with similes and images
that might have pleased John Donne, or Hart Crane if he had
found them. The following, for example, seems to us to be
as fine as Donne's celebrated ''twin compasses'':

Since first
my joy was all
your care,

I cannot
say "Love goes" without
distress.

To overlay
the tortoise shell
with gold

Makes outer
beauty for an inner
worthlessness.

[p. 103, above]

There are other poems in which she uses such images: she
speaks of the course of their affair, saying, "But, patterned
thread in a broken loom?" It is not just "showering petals
of spring," it is patterned thread in a broken loom: some-
thing very specific, like Homer's "As when some woman
stains ivory vermilion, to make it a cheekpiece for horses."*

Logopoeia

Logopoeia, including puns, is the part of any poetry that
translates least effectively. Tzu Yeh relies often enough on
logopoetic effect, but each instance is unique, or is so dif-
ficult to deal with, that we feel no "principles" can be for-
mulated. Much information on Tzu Yeh's puns and logo-
poeia, and on what we have tried to do to translate them,
can be found in our footnotes to the translated poems. The
following poem, from chapter 45 of the *Yueh-fu Shih-chi*,
often is taken to refer to Tzu Yeh's poetry and its style:

Guitars and flutes
        echo each phrase.
Clear sounds
        rest on steady drums.

* *Iliad* 4, 141–42; trans. W.M.

This singer
            has no studied style,
From her heart
            most moving music comes.

Tzu Yeh's "music" indeed is moving, but the line about "studied style" is as misleading as the tag "woodnotes wild" applied to Shakespeare. Anybody knows this who has read Sister Miriam Joseph, or tried to track down all Tzu Yeh's puns.

Method

Our actual "working method" was this: that Professor McNaughton should prepare "cribs" or literal versions, and that Miss Mayhew, after discussion, should find an accurate English equivalent poem. Although our responsibilities were divided in this way, we criticized each other's work continually as we went along, and often found this mutual criticism a stimulus as well as a corrective.

BIBLIOGRAPHY

This bibliography lists those books and articles which were most definitely and most directly useful to us as we translated the Tzu Yeh poems. We have omitted from the bibliography standard dictionaries and philological aids.

Chou Fa-kao: *Chung-kuo ku-tai yü-fa* [A Grammar of Classical Chinese]. 3 vols. Taipei, 1959, 1961, 1962.

———: "Reduplicatives in the Book of Odes," *Bulletin of the Institute of History and Philology of Academia Sinica* 34, no. 2 (1963).

Curtius, Ernst Robert: *Europäische Literatur und lateinisches Mittelalter*. Bern and Munich, 1948.

———: *European Literature and the Latin Middle Ages*. Translated by Willard Trask. Princeton, 1953.

Gourmont, Rémy de: *Esthétique de la langue française*. Paris, 1955.

Jacobson, Roman: "Linguistics and Poetics." In *Style in Language*. Edited by Thomas A. Sebeok. Cambridge, Mass., 1960.

Joseph, Sister Miriam: *Shakespeare's Use of the Arts of Language*. New York, 1949.

Karlgren, Bernhard: *Word Families in Chinese*. Stockholm, 1934.

Kennedy, George A.: *Selected Works*. Edited by Tien-yi Li. New Haven, 1964.

Liu Ta-chieh: *Chung-kuo wen-hsueh fa-chan shih* [A History of Chinese Literature and Its Development]. 3 vols. Hongkong, 1961.

Lu K'an-ju and Feng Yuan-chün: *Chung-kuo shih-shih* [A History of Chinese Poetry]. 3 vols. Peking, 1961.

McNaughton, William: "Chinese Poetry in Untranslation," *Delos* 1, no. 1 (1967).

————: "Pound's Translations and Chinese Melopoeia," *Texas Quarterly* 10, no. 4 (Winter 1967), pp. 52–56.

————: "Ezra Pound et la littérature chinoise," *L'Herne* 6, no. 2 (1965).

————: *Shih Ching Rhetoric: Schemes of Words*. Ann Arbor, 1967.

Oshanin, I. M., ed. *Nekotorye voprosy kitatskot grammatiki* [Some Problems in Chinese Grammar]. Moscow, 1957.

Pound, Ezra: *ABC of Reading*. Norfolk, Conn., n.d.

Scotellaro, Rocco. *È fatto giorno* [It's Day!]: *1940–1953*. Milan, 1954.

Valéry, Paul: *The Art of Poetry,* trans. Denise Folliot. New York, 1958.

————: *Variétés III*. Paris, 1936.

Van Gulik, R.H.: "Mi-hsi t'u-k'ao" [An Illustrated Investigation of the Secret Games; in English]. A photo-printed, 50-copy edition of the author's handwritten manuscript, available in some libraries.

Wang Li: *Han-yü shih-lü-hsueh* [Chinese Poetics]. Shanghai, 1962.

Wei-Chin Nan-pei-ch'au wen-hsueh-shih ts'an-k'ao tzu-liao [Materials for Studying the Literary History of the Wei and Chin Dynasties and of the Period of Division between the North and South]. Edited and annotated by the Chinese Literature Department of Peking University. 2 vols. Peking, 1962.

Wei Ch'ing-chih: *Shin-jen yü-hsueh* [Jade-filings from the Poets]. Shanghai, 1958.

Williams, William Carlos: *Collected Earlier Poems*. New York, 1951.

Yang Shu-ta: *Han-wen wen-yen hsiu-tz'u-hsueh* [Classical Chinese Rhetoric]. Peking, 1954.